The 21 Day Minimalism Challenge

Learn How to Simplify, Organize and Declutter Your Life

by
Olivia S. Taylor

Contents

Introduction

This book will begin with a simple assumption: that what happens in our external environments is reflected in our internal environments - in other words: chaos on the outside means chaos on the inside.

Think about it: everything you do - including the clothes you wear, the food you buy, the way you decorate your home - is a reflection of who you are as a person. If your world is disorganized, untidy or messy, chances are your thoughts and feelings are messy too.

Minimalism is an easy concept to understand. By clearing away everything that doesn't serve you, you make way for all those things that do serve you. When you clear away distractions and clutter in your outside world, your inner world gets a spring clean too.

What is cluttering up your life right now?

It may have taken you years to accumulate everything you have now, but if you are ready for a change it may only take 3 weeks to declutter your life once and for all. Seems impossible? Don't worry. Every journey starts with a single step, and by going step by step in this book we'll take a gradual path from clutter, chaos and disorganization to a home and lifestyle that is clear, clean and calm.

Each day you will find an exercise that you can do in your own life, right now. Reading about minimalism is well and good, but minimalism is something to do. With each new challenge, we'll move towards a more elegant and stream-lined life. Are you ready?

What is Minimalism?

*M*inimalism is about the essentials of life.

In recent years it has become fashionable to try and live with only 6 pieces of clothing, or to buy recipe books with as little as 3 ingredients per dish, or put a Zen garden in your back yard. But maybe it's best to think of what minimalism isn't.

It's not mindless consumption, and it's not clutter bought without any thought. It's not chaotic and rushed, it's not greedy or jealous. Minimalism is like a laser - it focuses energy and attention on one spot, making the rest irrelevant.

By living a more minimalist lifestyle, you invite calm and quiet into your daily life, you become more efficient, and you take action with more conviction than before. You don't fall prey to cheesy advertising, and you make your own goals. You think of money as a tool to reach your goals, and not the goal itself.

Being minimalist in today's world can feel a bit like swimming upstream. Our hope is that this book can be a good starting point, a catalyst and maybe even a kick in the pants. If you've had enough of chaos, mess and disorganization in your life, read on.

The Decision

Let's dive right in. Sometimes, the biggest problem when it comes to decluttering your life is not that you're busy or that you don't know how. It's that, in your heart, you haven't truly decided to turn over a new leaf.

Here is the first (and possibly most important) step you'll take towards your goals: decide to do it. Many people who begin a minimalist lifestyle get carried away with throwing things out. While we'll certainly be throwing things out (I bet you're thinking of something you want to throw out right now!) it's best to start with the psychological junk first.

What follows is a list of common excuses why people don't want to do what it takes to make a lifestyle change. Underneath every excuse is hidden fear and, yes, laziness. An excuse convinces you that you CAN'T do something, that it's not your fault, and oh well, you might as well just abandon your goal and go back to how things were.

See if you can find yourself in any of the following excuses:

- "I work full time and my house is only disorganized because I don't have time to fix it up! I'm not some kind of stay at home wife you know, I have a life."

- "Cleaning is just about the most boring thing I can think of. Minimalism sounds like such a nice idea - if only someone else could do it for me."

- "It's not so bad. Life is chaotic anyway, and there's nothing you can do about it. I mean, why make your bed when you're just going to sleep in it again?"

- "Oh I could never give up my second car/pile of rubbish under the bed/snow globe collection. I need it. I NEED IT."

- "I don't have excuses like those other people! I'm really going to change my lifestyle. I'll start by making a few lists and then I'll begin on Monday. Or Tuesday. Promise."

We could go into detail about what each of these excuses means, but the best way to deal with excuses is just to ignore them. Completely. If you have some reservations about living a simpler, more minimal lifestyle, if you're worried or feel like procrastinating, just ignore the impulse and move on. Don't embark on this project because you feel you should - do it because you want to.

Exercise for today: Find a small diary or journal and dedicate it to your 21 day challenge. On the first page, write the following:

Today, I am committed to a simpler, more minimalist lifestyle that truly serves me and my goals. No excuses.

Now, sign your name at the bottom. If you want to do it in blood on the evening of a full moon, go ahead - do whatever you need to to convince yourself that the decision is made, and is final.

Congratulations, you've made your first step towards a simpler lifestyle. If you feel your resolve wavering, come back to your "contract" and read it again. Doesn't it feel good to let go of old excuses?

Day 2

Smart Planning

They say a goal without a plan is just a wish. Now that you've committed to making a significant change in your life, the next step is to make (smart) plans about how you're going to get where you want to go.

I recommend reading through this entire book first to get a sense of the process before embarking on your own plan. This way you can get a feel of what to expect and you avoid starting something that might turn out to be difficult to finish later down the line.

Now, although the book is organized into 21 days to make things more structured and simpler, there's no rule that you have to follow the process perfectly and in 21 days. You've made the commitment, now you need to be realistic about what will fit for your life. Here are some things to think about:

1. How much time do you have? You will just demotivate yourself if you try to do a complete life overhaul when realistically you only have 30 free minutes everyday. Be honest about how much time you have to commit. If it makes sense for you to do a "daily" exercise every 3 days or even every week, it makes no difference, as long as the pace works for you and most importantly gets you to your goals.

2. When do you want to start? It's tempting to just jump right in but be smart about when you choose to begin. Starting over a holiday period or a long weekend is a good idea since you'll have the time to do it

properly. Make sure you don't have any big projects or events at the time that can distract you.

3. What will you do with all the things you no longer need? Be conscientious. You might no longer have room in your life for something, but that doesn't mean someone else can't make use of it. Think about what to do with extra stuff - sell it online? Have a garage sale? Donate it to charities or second hand shops? Give it away? Throw it away?

4. How are you going to keep track of your progress? If you wrote down your "contract" in a small journal, this is the perfect place to jot down plans, goals and notes for each day. Even if your house is so chaotic it feels like you want to scream just thinking about it, having a nice, neat little journal can be calming and a good way to organize your thoughts. Decide how you're going to keep track of and record your minimalism adventure. Will you record your thoughts and feelings, too?

Day 3

Putting on Minimalist Glasses

Living an organized, minimalist lifestyle is all about attitude.

Though you might be glad to finally toss out all those magazines you've been holding onto for years, the real change with minimalism happens inside your head. So learn to start looking at things like a minimalist, be curious about the role that different items play in your life. And well, be a little ruthless too.

Do this exercise with a random item in your house, right now (yes, right now!). Have a good look at it.

- Could you live without this item?

- Could you live *happily* without this item?

- What was your life like before you had it?

- How often do you use it - honestly?

- Will you keep using it?

- Does this item make you happy?

- Is this item beautiful?

- Does this item stress you out and cost money to maintain?

- Why did you buy this item?

- Do you already something better to replace this item?

- If you don't use it, why do you keep it?

- What emotions do you have for this item - fear, sentimentality, obligation or expectation?

- Would your life improve without it?

And lastly (and this is the most important question of all): What is this item's *value*?

This doesn't mean the amount of money you paid for it. This means how much value it adds to your life, whether it is useful or makes you happy, whether it helps you be the person you want to be. Go as deep with this exercise as you want, but for the next 21 days, try to get used to "seeing" things for their real value.

Day 4

Whipping the Kitchen Into Shape

L et's not linger on the philosophy. *Time for action!*

The kitchen is a great place to start - it's busy, it's prominent in everyone's schedule... and it's usually the most disorganized.

Yesterday, you tried looking at the things you own with a new perspective - today you're going to put that into practice. Start at one end of the kitchen and move across. Look at your fridge, the appliances in your cupboards, your pantry, your crockery and drawers. What does a minimalist kitchen look like? Well, that depends on you.

If you've been a health junky for years, it's obvious you shouldn't lose your juicer and if you barely eat at home and are an awful cook, a 12 piece pot and pan set is possible a bit of a waste. Be careful of getting trapped in the "should" frame of mind. Often our actual lifestyles and the lifestyle we wish we had are miles apart. Maybe you're holding onto that pasta machine you never use because in your mind, all serious cooks should own one and you really want to think of yourself as a serious cook. Maybe you keep a juicer because it makes you feel like a healthy person (even though you've only used it once). Maybe you realize it was a bad buy but you feel guilty now and might as well keep it.

Be ruthless. Throw away old jars of fancy ingredients you bought to make one special meal months ago and never used since. Throw out that strange box of dried beans. Do you really need that container of rubber bands in the bottom drawer? Throw out broken and expired things. Watch how much more space appears as you do. Feeling energetic? Might as well deep-clean the cupboards and fridge while you're at it!

Day 5

Cleaning Out Your closet

How did yesterday go? Make a note in your journal. Did you give up halfway, cry when you had to get rid of something sentimental or procrastinate the whole thing? Make a note. If you understand your own resistance, you can deal with it better when it rears its ugly head. Next to the kitchen, the closet easily becomes clogged with things you don't want, like or need. Let's dive in.

For this exercise you'll need 3 big boxes labeled "stays", "goes" and "not sure yet". Now, take everything - and I mean everything - out of your closet and lay it down somewhere clean, your bed for instance. Put on your minimalist glasses and go through each and every item. Depending on the size of your closet you might need a few hours, but the sense of relief you feel afterwards is well worth it, I promise.

Think of your clothes as going through special elimination rounds - only the best remain, and the rest are voted out.

The first question

Have you worn it in the last year? If not, put it aside for now, this item doesn't go into the "stays" box.

The second question

Ok, so you've worn it a few times. Next question: Does this item fit? Here, I'm using fit in a very general sense. Does it fit your body of course, but does it also fit your life? Maybe you're a businesswoman now and have no need for towering plastic stripper heels anymore. Maybe you're looking at a pair of pants that always, always pinches at the back and puts you in a bad mood. Maybe you bought that jacket when you lived in a colder place and now you never wear it anymore. If it doesn't fit, it "goes". If it fits, put in the box marked "stays".

The third question

When you've gone through all of your clothes it's time to take a honest look at the items that you haven't worn in a year. Some items can go the "goes" box without any effort, but what about that expensive jacket? Those pretty tops and all the clothes that you want to wear once you lose weight? Be really honest with yourself, if you haven't worn it in a year you most likely won't wear it in the next year either, which means it's just sitting around sapping your energy and taking up space. Let go if you can, but don't beat yourself up if it's too hard. Put the items that require some more time to say goodbye to in the "not sure yet" box.

Now take everything in the "stays" box and pack it into your wardrobe again (if you have the time, clean out the inside before you do). The "goes" box can go to friends, family, charity or the second hand shop. The "not sure yet" box can be put aside, but mark a day one month from now in your diary to reassess those items.

Day 6

House Raid 1

Your first big decluttering.

Think of this as a kind of therapy - as you throw away things you don't need, enjoy the feeling of becoming clear-headed, less stressed and calmer. It can be incredibly relieving to clear away dirt and junk from your life, and all you need is a big garbage bag, a box and your new minimalist glasses.

Keeping in mind your goals, go room to room and take out everything that you obviously don't need anymore. Throw away the rubbish and put the items that can be of value for other people in the box. Err on the side of taking out more: if you are unsure and it doesn't upset you too much you get rid of the item. More often than not, being unsure about something is a sign that you're holding onto what you think the thing gives you, rather than its true value. Think of all those things in your life that you love. You can identify them quickly and easily, and wouldn't dream of giving them away. That's the attitude you need to have for everything in your life eventually.

Obviously, you'll need to keep the practical things that nobody can live without. Your toothbrush, curtains, a place to sit etc. Nobody would argue about these things. But don't take your own word for it if you quickly decide "oh well, I need that". Need is relative. Making your life more minimalist means adjusting your concept of need.

A house raiding tip: if you live in a place for a long time, you start to not really notice it anymore. To you, that pile of papers on the end of your desk more or less... disappears. Get some fresh eyes to help you find these "blind spots". Invite a good friend over and get their help if you're having difficulty identifying clutter. What do they notice that you may have stopped noticing? You might be shocked how much you have become accustomed to!

Day 7

Letting Go

So what was yesterday like?

As we've already seen, the items in our lives can so often be much more than just items. The fact is, we live in a world where items become infused with meaning, and where those items become part of our identities and memories.

As you went through your things yesterday, you probably stumbled on a few items that had you feeling conflicted. Everybody has items like this in their lives. A trophy from a spelling bee you won thirty years ago. A gift from an ex wife. An expensive silk dress that is the most beautiful thing you've ever owned - but never worn. What on earth do you do with these things?

Let it go!

Watch yourself and how you respond emotionally to an object. If something hasn't been used for years (or ever!) and actually has no function in your life, but you still keep it around, it must be for a reason. A good clue that an item is serving an emotional function is that you feel a strong emotional reaction to getting rid of it. Think about it. Your spelling bee trophy may be a cheap plastic trinket that's worth nothing at all, but to you, it may represent the last time you felt proud of your achievements. To you, that silly trophy could be wrapped up in your feelings of self worth, in memories of your childhood and complicated emotions around who you are as a person, about winning, about life.

In other words, it's not just a *thing*.

Here's the truth though: your emotion and the things are not the same. Throw away the junk and you still have your memories. Get rid of the memento, the keepsake or the knick knack and you still have the emotion and the feeling you attached to it.

Of course, nobody would suggest you throw away things that make you happy. But, many people hold onto junk and clutter because it's a shortcut to holding onto the emotions behind them. This is the difference between keeping a beautiful photograph of your grandmother and holding on to boxes and boxes of the junk she left in your house after she died.

Today's exercise: What serves you? This is difficult stuff. Be patient with yourself.

Day 8

Finding Your Own Minimalism

Well, let's take a step back from the therapy for a moment and get a bit more practical.

Today, you'll try let go of ideas of minimalism itself that are not serving you. Too often, minimalism seems like some kind of punishment. Like something you do to balance out overindulgence, a life diet almost.

The name "minimalism" is kind of a bad one. It suggests having only a little. It almost suggests poverty. But this is wrong. Minimalism will look different for everyone. Why? Because what serves each of us is different. Minimalism is about finding out what things in your life are important and what things are not - and then structuring your life so that you focus on those things that serve you and get rid of those that don't.

Today will be a journaling day. If you're not comfortable journaling, just meditate on some of these concepts before continuing. If you find that you're forcing yourself to throw away things, you're doing it wrong. Minimalism should suit you. So... what's your particular brand of minimalism?

What items are really important to you?

Some people care about luxurious clothes or electronics and others couldn't be bothered. Maybe you're the kind of person who needs high end cosmetics but doesn't care in the least about fancy shoes or special kitchen appliances. It's up to you.

What items don't you care about?

Spending money and energy on things that bring you no pleasure makes no sense. Maybe everyone in your peer group owns a particular thing. But is that a good enough reason for you to have one also?

What is your personal minimum?

Enough is not too little. It's enough. How much is enough for you?

Day 9

Digital De-Cluttering

I have a friend who looks like a minimalist. He has very little furniture in his home, wears simple clothes and more or less lives like a nomad. Try to pry his MacBook away from him though, and I believe he'll suffer a cardiac arrest there and then.

Technology is a wonderful thing, but at the end of the day it's also a "thing".

As our lives are increasingly lived out in virtual spaces, more and more of our clutter becomes the virtual kind. Are you one of those people who has a spotless home but thousands of backed up emails since 1999 and every episode of Friends on your hard drive?

Let it go!

1. Streamline your email. Unsubscribe from newsletters you always delete anyway and clear out your spam folder.

2. Organize your filing system - have clear folders for all your separate documents, get rid of loose ends and random things you haven't looked at in years. Get help from a tech-savvy person who won't snoop around in your browser history.

3. Got a dead Twitter account with nothing in it? Delete it. Same for any other profiles or social media pages you never use.

4. If you have a few separate email addresses, try to reroute everything so it comes to one place. Decide on a time each day as well as a time limit to check your email. Email can be a huge stressor and time-sink. Check it once or twice a day and then let it go.

5. It's hard, but get rid of games that you find yourself losing hours of your life playing. Addictive games are like brain clutter.

6. Give yourself a Facebook diet. Decide on the maximum amount of time you're willing to devote to socializing everyday on Facebook, then stop.

7. Unless you're some kind of day trader who works on Wall Street and risks losing thousands of dollars unless he checks his email this very second, then get rid of notifications on your phone. They're distracting and addictive. Avoid looking at your phone all the time. Is there not something interesting happening in the real world?

8. If you've been procrastinating on doing those software updates or need new anti-virus updates, do it now. You might like to get rid of any programs and applications that take up space and never get used.

9. Comb through old photos and get rid of ones you don't care about and organize the rest. You might like to, ahem, keep a locked and secure folder for anything private.

10. Lastly, get hold of a laptop cleaner. Turn everything off and go over it with a soft cloth. Keyboards especially can get really filthy. Clean off the smears on your iPad, put a new screen cover on your phone and wipe off those earphones.

Day 10

Simplify Your Diet

We are more or less halfway into our minimalism journey. By now, it should be getting easier to know what is serving you in life and what is just taking up space. Our next step? Simplifying eating habits.

Nowhere are we bombarded with more messages about what we should do than with diet. You know the story: a health guru tells you carbs are poison. Your neighbor won't shut up about juice cleanses. Your mom says you need to eat more. Suddenly everyone's eating wheatgrass again. It gets confusing.

Luckily you, gentle reader, have a powerful tool to guide you through this nonsense. In the same way you're getting used to asking whether things serve you, you can ask whether food is really doing you any good.

- How does a certain food make you feel?

- What do you really like to eat?

- When are you hungry, and how often?

- How much food do you really need?

Today's exercise will be to start learning to listen to your body. If you aren't hungry, don't eat. If you're craving something, eat it (of course, you need to listen to your body afterwards too... you might feel like three slices of cheesecake would serve you very well indeed, but then notice that you feel sick afterwards and make the relevant adjustments).

Let go of "shoulds" and eating rules. Eat for yourself.

Food clutter can take on many forms. It could be that horrible collection of unused spices in the back of your pantry, a nasty habit of eating cookies every day after dinner or the raw vegan diet you think you should be happy on but just aren't. Try to keep up your new minimalist diet for the rest of the 21 days. Is it really such a big deal to skip a meal, for example?

Day 11

Honing in on Life Goals

So far we've thrown around this idea of what serves you, what enables you to live your best life. The idea is that if only you could remove the clutter, the mess and the distractions, your true happiness and purpose would emerge from underneath. Sounds great, right?

But the more you think about this idea, the more you'll see that removing clutter from your life forces you to ask yourself some important questions: what are you actually doing? What's the point of it all? What do you really want?

The thing is, a life of distraction prevents you from ever focusing on these questions. Remove the distractions and you might find yourself stressing over these bigger-picture issues all of a sudden. And here you thought you were just going to tidy up a little!

It's inevitable. You start by asking whether you should keep your collection of rare comics from your childhood. To decide whether they're valuable or not though, you'll need a clear idea of what they add to your life. To do that you'll need to know what makes you happy in the first place.

I recommend getting rid of them and working out the details later, but here is an exercise to help you zoom in on what really matters to you - that *one* thing that helps you make all your other decisions. Your compass.

In your journal, note down *three of the best experiences in your entire life.* They can be anything. If you like, close your eyes and really try to put yourself back in that moment. Smell the smells, remember the sounds, tastes and feelings. Now, make a note of what exactly made that moment special.

Was it the feeling of bliss and freedom at having done something new and different? Was it the warm sense of love for someone close to you? Something spiritual? Did it involve nature, or food, or learning? See if there's anything in common between the three experiences. You're beginning to get an idea of what makes you tick at your core.

If you discover that one thing that gives your life meaning and color, wouldn't you want to make sure that all your actions enabled more of that in the future? How silly is it to spend so much time on the nonsense and drudgery of life when you could be working towards creating more memories like this?

Now, when you look at an item, ask yourself if it's going to help or hinder you on your way to what's really important.

Day 12

House Raid 2

With that in mind, it's time for another house raid.

Whereas your first house raid was a practical exercise focused on getting rid of, to put it plainly, all the crap in your house, your second house raid is going to be a little more subtle. One of the ideas with minimalism is that if you can remove all the useless rubbish clogging your daily life, you can more clearly see the important things underneath.

This time, as you go through your house, put on your minimalist glasses and ask yourself - *does this serve me?*

Let's say you have a beautiful vintage crystal bowl that your husband bought you for an anniversary a few years ago. You used it once and then it sat in your kitchen cupboard ever since. Take a good, hard look at this bowl and try to see it for what it is.

Perhaps, after thinking about it for a while, you realize that every time you look at this bowl you feel bad about yourself. You get a wave of guilt and obligation - this bowl, after all, is what you would use if you were a more sophisticated domestic goddess type, if you actually had guests over like a mature grown up instead of just meeting friends at the pub once in a while. Maybe this bowl is even something that belongs to the kind of woman your husband actually prefers, and maybe he wants you to be more like that?

How could you get rid of something so valuable and beautiful and expensive anyway? Maybe you'll use it eventually. Maybe you should just plan an elaborate dinner party one day so you can use it already. The trouble is, you hate hosting dinner parties. You hate cooking. Without even knowing it, you have a mild existential breakdown every time you open your kitchen cupboard and catch a glimpse of that glinting crystal gathering dust in the back.

The bowl, though it might be a thing of beauty for someone else, only makes you feel awful about your life and who you are. Some people build their entire lives around things they think they should want. Some people, in other words, live in worlds made entirely of beautiful crystal bowls.

Your exercise for today: do a house raid as you did before, only this time, ask whether an item serves you. How does it make you feel? Do you feel comforted, energized or entertained by it? Does it inspire you, keep you safe or make you feel amazing in any way?

Day 13

Some Soul Searching

Think of this as *reverse retail therapy.*

Today is going to be a day where you turn inward a little more and start focusing on what lies beneath the clutter. Here a bit of a warning: as we've seen, things can become so much more than things when we infuse them with meaning, with our identities, with hopes and dreams and fears and obligations.

When you remove the things, expect that all the emotions that thing was helping to hide will come flooding back out again. Imagine a mother who feels bad about not spending enough time with her children. For her, the piles and piles of unused toys are evidence that, at least in some ways, she is in fact doing her job as a parent. If she cleared away that clutter, suddenly that feeling of unfulfilled responsibilities could come back. She may say, almost irrationally, that her kids "need" those toys and feel a mild sense of panic at the idea that she should throw them out.

You may have something like this in your life, or you may simply have a home that's been a little neglected over the years. In any case, try to use the following questions to hone in on what's behind the way you buy things, own things, and throw things away.

- Why do you buy the things you do - is it because of advertising, pressure from friends, envy of others or even as stress relief? If you feel like you "should" buy it, why? What would happen if you didn't?

- What kind of lifestyle do you actually have and what kind of lifestyle is served by the things you own? Maybe everyone tells you that your home should look a certain way, but when you look carefully at how you actually live, it doesn't make sense to have a home like that.

- Are there any social and cultural pressures that you feel duty-bound to follow? Is the pleasure you get from complying more than the pleasure you'd get from going your own way?

- Do the things in your life generally help you along to your goals or do they only get in your way?

- Look at your home and your lifestyle like a stranger would. What kind of person lives there? Is this really an accurate picture of who you are?

- When you were little, what excited you the most about life?

- Lastly, ask yourself how you think about money and success. Are they the same thing?

Day 14

Time Commitments

As you can see, we're starting to look at more and more things with minimalist glasses. Eventually, those glasses become permanent and you begin to see the world in a different light entirely. In truth, how organized and streamlined your house becomes is just a symptom of an organized and streamlined mind.

Your lifestyle manifests in the things you own, but it's also in the way you spend your time. In other words, you may have a slick, clean home but a schedule that's full of wasted time, obligations and nonsense. Today, let's start spring cleaning the way we use time.

Addictions

Just try add up the hours you sacrifice to watching TV series every evening. Hour by hour, that's your life you're wasting. Computer games that suck you in, Facebooking even when it only makes you grumpy, surfing the net reading things you don't care about but can't pull yourself away from... you get the idea. Imagine the possibilities if you took those hours and put them to use doing something that served you instead.

Draining relationships

Of course, people aren't things. But relationships can be healthy or unhealthy, and some relationships have more or less the same effect on you as that pile of rubbish in your garden shed. Do you have anyone in your life that takes but never gives? Someone that makes you feel bad about yourself every time you're with them? Think of it this way: every moment you spend with someone who doesn't serve you, you're missing out on the chance to be with someone that does.

Obligations

Your boss wants you to come to an (unpaid) work function for the third time this month. Your neighbors are pestering you to join the PTA. Your church group thinks you should organize the bake sale. Your distant cousin wants you to fly to another city for her wedding. This is clutter - only social clutter.

In life, we all make compromises, and part of being a social animal is occasionally taking part in rituals that we don't necessarily enjoy. But if you're not getting a net gain, there's something wrong. Remember, you are the only one who has to live with your life. You have some duties to others, but at some point, if it doesn't bring you joy, then why are you doing it?

For today's exercise, go back and look at your schedule for the past week. What could have been "thrown out"? What served you and what didn't? Deciding on what your own personal level of obligation to friends and family is can be one of the most empowering things you can do.

Day 15

Your Car

For many people, their car is a bit like an extension of their house, and forms a big part of their life. This varies a lot, as people in different countries have very different car cultures and different options when it comes to public transport.

What about you?

First of all, do you even really need a car? In sprawling American suburbs, a car is essential, but in smaller urban European cities, a car is completely unnecessary and even a bit of a hindrance. Compare the cost of a monthly car payment and gas with how much you'd spend on public transport. Factor in how much time you'd gain/lose.

If you do need a car, do you really need the one you have? Most people have a car with two back seats that never get used. If you only use it for short trips, does it need to be that big and fancy? Many people balk at the idea, but would you actually save money by getting an older, second hand model instead?

On a related note, smartphones can be thought of much the same way. "Because I thought it was cool" is not the best reason to get the newest iPhone for example. Maybe you love getting new upgrades every few months, but on looking closer you realize your phone plan is expensive and unnecessary.

Day 16

The House

What is your house, really, but a big vehicle that carries you through your life in general?

Quickly, imagine that as you move around your home, you leave a visible trail behind you. Over the course of the month, where would most of these trails accumulate? If you have a room where you barely go, you would lose nothing by moving to a house without that room. In fact, you'd likely save money.

Extra space in your home means extra cleaning, extra things you need to buy to fill up that space, extra rent etc. *Do you really need it?*

What about your garden? Do you have too much or not enough wardrobe space? Do you ever use that storage room? How much of your kitchen do you actually use? Do you entertain a lot or is that huge dinner table wasted?

Going bigger still, what about the area the house is in? Does this neighborhood serve your needs? What about the city you live in or even the country? The thing about big, scary decisions like moving house is that they count as many, many smaller decisions all at once. If you move to another city, you could get rid of your car, move to a smaller place you enjoy, and completely change your lifestyle in one fell swoop.

Day 17

Minimalist Shopping Habits

Hurray for you! You've cleaned up your home, asked yourself some tricky questions and started to make moves towards what really matters in your life. Now, let's keep it that way. Hopefully, in the past few days you've managed to undo years and years - even a lifetime - of habits and conditioning. But the next step is to make sure that you carry this new perspective with you into the future.

How to shop like a minimalist

Choose the right time to go shopping. Go when you're hungry, tired, sad or stressed and you'll probably fall prey to horrible advertising and end up buying things you don't want or need. Don't give yourself the chance to impulse buy. Make a plan and stick to it, then go when the shops are quiet and you have plenty of time to make smart decisions.

Most advertising works by convincing you that a particular item will give you a particular lifestyle. This is backwards. Resist the urge to go along with the illusion and instead ask yourself how an item really fits into your life. What does this piece of clothing match with in your closet? How often will you use this gadget? What will you actually make with this kitchen appliance?

Look for **quality**. Make sure that when you buy something, you're buying it to last. Check the seams and trimmings on clothes. Understand guarantees and warranties. Look closely for defects. How long will this thing last? Is it really worth the price?

For bigger purchases, don't buy immediately. Go home, think it over. If you still think it's a good idea after a night's sleep, go ahead and get it.

Think carefully if, in a way, you don't already own the thing you're shopping for. Sounds strange, but many people buy the same item of clothing over and over, or a million bottles of the same reddish nail polish. Somewhere in your life is something you bought in the past and got excited about. Look for it.

Do you even need to buy the thing new? Sometimes, you can get amazing second hand items for a fraction of the price. Join clothing or makeup exchanges, visit second hand shops or scour online forums for deals.

Day 18

Collect Moments, Not Things

You don't lose the memory when you lose the memento that reminded you of it. Things with "sentimental value" can be tricky, because they can be like keys to past experiences. This means throwing your deceased dog's old collar away is like throwing away the memory itself. How could you possibly do it?

Minimalists are not masochists - nobody would argue that keeping around one or two special photographs, heirlooms or gifts doesn't have immense value. But what is valuable is what they point to - the feelings they stir up, the memories they jog. Why not just focus on those feelings directly?

As you go through life, consider collecting moments, experiences and connections with others instead of material things. For your gifts to others, buy an experience they can enjoy or you can share with them. Bungee jumping, cooking classes, a massage, a trip to the ballet, a camping trip or tickets to a festival are all incredibly life-enriching without physically cluttering up your space.

They say you can't take it all with you. On your deathbed, which would satisfy you more - a house full of things or the memory of a lifetime full of meaningful experiences shared with people you care about?

Day 19

Work and Finances

T he cool thing about trading in your clutter for actual human experiences is that you usually get quite a good deal. When you spend less money, you don't need as much money, and when you don't need as much money, you don't need to work as much. I'm sure you can think of people you know who seem to earn double what you do and yet still stress about money, still seem to never have enough. When they get a raise, they just ramp up their lifestyle to match and soon they're merely scraping by again.

Once you start living with a more streamlined, minimalist life philosophy, you may be surprised at how little you actually need. The typical Western lifestyle uses things and money as a stand-in for happiness. Celebrations and holidays are about gifts. We sell our weekdays in exchange for money and then blow all that money on the weekend trying to recapture the sense of well being we lost by working so hard in the first place.

When you make a regular budget, it's about squeezing the most out of every penny. When you're a minimalist though, it's about squeezing the most out of your life. You could probably get away with budget toilet paper and rice and beans for dinner to save money, but what's it all worth if you're not happy?

- Could you work less? Can your job be converted to a part time position, could you get more vacation time or could you work from home occasionally?

- Do you have "work clutter" in your home life? Look carefully to see if you carry work with you wherever you go. What are you missing by constantly being in work mode?

- On the other hand, is it time to lose the lower paying job and start pushing for more money?

- What bad work habits and toxic relationships can you let go of?

- Could you be delegating some work to others so you can focus on more interesting or challenging aspects?

- Are you effectively managing your time? Automate as much as you can.

Day 20

Repurposing Your Time

So, you've cleared up your home of clutter and mess. You've figured out, at least in some way, what makes you happy and what doesn't. You've had a look at your spending habits, your job, and your relationships with others. Congratulations - you've taken the first steps to building the lifestyle you want, from the ground up.

We all have different resources (some people, unfortunately, have way more resources than others!) but one thing we all have is a fixed amount of time. We all get 24 hours. Eventually, we all die.

How is it that some people create fabulous, colorful lives, build powerful companies or business empires, nurture epic families or launch new ideas into the world ...while other people work like mad but can't seem to find an hour at the end of their day for a Zumba class?

The answer is priorities.

Do you think Steve Jobs cared about keeping a home that would impress his neighbors while growing up? Did Cleopatra throw away 2 hours of every day watching ancient Egypt's equivalent of Jersey Shore? Did Gandhi stress that the guys at work would think his cellphone was outdated?

When you know what is important to you, you can devote more of your time to it. Every moment you spend not pursuing those things that make you happy and fulfilled is a moment lost forever. Coming up with something as intimidating as a "life purpose" is pretty hard, but it's easy to move away from things that leave you tired, sad, angry and uninspired and towards things that make you feel alive.

Sure, almost everybody needs to work, pay taxes, make a budget. But these things should be in service of your life, they shouldn't become your life. Forget about all the things that have happened before. What is important to you, right now, in this moment? And what can you do that will bring you closer and closer to that?

Day 21

Minimalist Tips and Tricks

You're on your last day.

But really, you're at the start of potentially something new. If you want, this could be the first day of a whole new way of thinking about yourself, your life, your things. Life is short, so here are some quick tips to whip out as you navigate this cluttered and chaotic world:

1. Become good at conversions. When you see the price of something, convert it into something else. How much time does this thing cost? What other things could you buy for the same money? A price tag of $100 might not seem like much until you consider that it represents 4 whole hours of your life. Is it worth it now?

2. Learn to say no. Over-consuming is easy. Turn down the second helping, politely decline taking on extra work, say no to advertising when it tells you your life won't be complete without their product. Just say no. It gets easier!

3. Resist carrying too much cash with you and make it a routine to wait at least 24 hours before making bigger purchases.

4. At different moments throughout the day, make a habit of asking yourself the value of what you're doing. How could you best use each moment?

5. Give yourself a TV or Internet limit and stick to it.

6. Get used to doing "nothing". Take up meditation. Sit and watch the birds in the trees. Not every moment must be filled. Curiously, you may feel more fulfilled by doing "nothing" than you do constantly filling yourself up with noise and clutter.

7. Keep up journaling. Remind yourself of the bigger picture. Be patient.

8. Choose one or two days a week where you buy nothing at all. Stay out of the shops. Maybe go out into nature. See how full life is without an overabundance of material things.

9. Get crafty. Learning how to make things gives you a new appreciation and perspective for them. Creating things is an amazing antidote to mindlessly consuming them. Mend and fix things you think are useless. Recycle and repurpose things to bring them to life again - after all, this is exactly the way Mother Nature herself works.

Conclusion

*N*ow what?

Good question. It's up to you. On the surface, this is a simple book that is all about organizing your life, de-cluttering and generally cleaning up your act. But I hope that along the way, you've discovered some things about yourself that you can take beyond the 21 days. Minimalism is about getting to the roots of things, and it will be different for everyone. But in our increasingly competitive and materialistic world, we could all learn to take a deep breath, take a step back and adjust our perspective.

I don't know what your personal minimalism looks like, but our hope is that from here on, you find yourself becoming more and more familiar with it. An elegant and purposeful life can take decades to create, but on the other hand, it really can be as simple as throwing out that clutter and changing your mindset. Just let it go.

Other 21-Day Challenges you may enjoy!

All challenges are available in Paperback, eBook and Audiobook format

Self-Love

Confidence

Happiness

Mindfulness

Stress Management

Exercise

Weight Loss

Clean Eating

Minimalism

Budgeting

Love Collection – 3 Books: Self-Love, Confidence & Happiness

Complete Collection – 10 Books